*Praise for* **SHIN YU PAI**

"Open your heart and read. These are words uttered in search of right speech, not just the poet's but our own: 'claim this / beauty that belongs to you / and make it yours.'" — Thomas Hitoshi Pruiksma

"*Virga* is a plate of pearls, each shining and singing in its own melody. Reading Pai's poetry requires 'single minded focus.' We have no choice but to look inward, learning how to 'bend w/out breaking.' That is exactly what poetry does for us, and what Shin Yu Pai has done for us with her dry rain." — Wang Ping

"The defining aspect of the lockdown era is our daily recalibration of the psyche. Shin Yu Pai's *Virga* shows us how assembling our sense of identity – from scraps of memory, travel, tradition, parenting, and always, always love – is an act of soul retrieval. We are cloudbursts forever becoming better cloudbursts. It doesn't matter when we rain." — Tom Gilroy

"Wittgenstein said that where one can speak, one must speak clearly. Where one cannot speak, one must be silent. Shin Yu Pai's collection *Virga* speaks eloquently of silences and the places where wisdom materializes." — Koon Woon

"Tranquility spreads through the poems in *Virga*. Raindrops restrain themselves from landing, or branches from leafing. The most enchanting moment in traversing through the scenes gathered here is to reconfigure lines on facing pages and create a third dimension – an emptiness that is said can only be reached with years of practice. Superstitious Asians vs. Imprints; Cloisters vs. The pearl diver's tale. One can read them as two discrete poems or a single work crossing vast spans of human conditions. In the end, we, the readers, 'with twin clarity / such that you / who are nothing but ears, / arrive wide awake.'" — Zhang Er, author of *First Mountain*

"In *Virga*, Shin Yu Pai searches for a way to combine the demands of contemporary life with a search for community in the competing worlds of Buddhist and literary practice. To build that bridge, she draws on sources as different as the haiku tradition and the talk poems of David Antin."
— Rae Armantrout

"Pai continually transforms the challenges she encounters — deaths, losses, disappointments — into opportunities to become closer to life, to what is important, what is joyous, what is wise: the best parts of being human."
— Page Hill Starzinger, *On The Seawall*

"One of the most thoughtful poets in the Northwest."
— Paul Constant, *Seattle Review of Books*

"Filled with luster, gleaming with deep insight, and further characterized by an ethereal landscape, focused on emotional connections, on spirituality, on death, and on the afterlife. Pai's work travels both within and outside of ethnic and racial frames, thus complicating any transparent categorization... as 'Asian American' literature." — Stephen Hong Sohn

"Her lines...unfold in layers of syntax and pauses that force the reader to consider each one as if it were complete unto itself, each line a jewel in an individual setting." — *International Examiner*

"A testament to the notion that meditation is not merely an emptying of the mind, but an active cultivation of being by being among things... to cultivate a thoughtful pose, which certainly is the foundation for an ethically lived existence." — *Hyphen Magazine*

"In Pai's figuration...the practice of art is the solution for living a life as elegant as the art object itself." — Joyelle McSweeney, *Constant Critic*

"Engagement with things in Pai counteracts the foreign objecthood usually ascribed to both the avante-garde art object in particular and Asianness in general." — Joseph Jonghyun Jeon, *Racial Things, Racial Forms: Objecthood in Avant-Garde Asian American Poetry*

"Pai presents small details as points of entry into ambitious questions about time and history, suggesting the impossibility of creating simple cause and effect relationships when each image, each landscape, and each piece of ephemera contains worlds." — Kristina Marie Darling, *Colorado Review*

# VIRGA

# VIRGA

## SHIN YU PAI

EMPTY BOWL

Anacortes, Washington

ISBN 978-1-7370408-0-4
Library of Congress Control Number: 2021936775

EMPTY BOWL
14172 Madrona Drive
Anacortes, WA 98223
www.emptybowl.org
emptybowl1976@gmail.com

Available from your local bookstore, emptybowl.org,
SPD, Ingram, Amazon, Barnes & Noble.

Printed at Gray Dog Press, Spokane, WA.
Cover art by April Gornik, *Virga*, 1992, oil on linen,
Smithsonian American Art Museum, Gift of the James F. Dicke Family,
2013.88.4, © 1992, April Gornik.
Author photo by Arzente Fine Art.
Interior author image by Joshua Huston.
Cover & book design by Lauren Grosskopf.

Empty Bowl, founded in 1976 as a cooperative letterpress publisher, has produced
periodicals, broadsides, literary anthologies, collections of poetry, and books of
Chinese translations. As of 2018, our mission is to publish the work of writers
who share Empty Bowl's founding purpose, "literature and responsibility," and its
fundamental theme, the love and preservation of human communities in wild places.

## Acknowledgments

Earlier versions of these poems appeared in *AIR | LIGHT, Behind a Door, Town Crier, ANMLY, The Chrysanthemum Review, Hobart, Lights, Pageboy, eMerge Magazine, Seattle Review of Books,* the *WA129* anthology project, and the 2019 *Till* chapbook.

"Star shine" was written as part of an artist-in-residency at the Pacific Science Center. It also exists as a poem video made by David Ian Bickley.

"Ashide no yo" appeared in *Spirited Stone* from Chin Music Press.

"Cloisters" and "The pearl diver's tale" appeared as limited-edition book arts projects from Editions Press in 2020.

"Embarkation" was commissioned by Forterra for Ampersand Live! in 2019 and published in *Genealogy 2020 4(3)*.

"Anything can go wrong, at any time" was written for and performed at the *Cascadian Zen* conference hosted at Seattle University in 2020.

# TABLE OF CONTENTS

*Empty Zendo*

for Bill Scheffel

when is the hall never not vacant?

alone in my cottage
I think of my teacher

gone now two years

straining to hear
the sound of the inverted bell

a Tibetan bowl sings

while I study the interiors
of other human habitations

transmitted over computer cams
the sangha divided now

more than ever I will practice
for as long as I am able

*Rōhatsu*

next year *I will fast*
*first* I say to my partner,

feeling shame for having
taken a hot shower &

shrouding myself
in lambswool. I am not

austere enough to enter
any cave I think instead

of embarking on that diet
of nettles for weeks

my skin is frequently green
from envy. I am swaddled

in blankets as I turn out
the lights strike a match

to light the flame
take a seat to meet

the gathering darkness
of my many selves

*Being Avalokiteshvara*

is not no
sweat, right
speech aside,

all so goddamn effortless

no matter, what
the amateurs say, vows
ain't bragging rights

if I had a thousand arms
if I had a thousand eyes

action would still ask single-
minded focus, I am no less

a goddess, with this one
pair of hands, these waning

eyes, looking inward as I realize
how to bend w/out breaking

*Where you go*

beyond
the palace walls

of the mind

see the half-clothed
child at the roadside stand

hear the howl
of street dogs

that keep you
awake at night

to be born

these words
rising in me

I say for all
living beings

*The gift*

In another land
I ask permission to take
from the fig tree.

My guide says
the Bhutanese believe
plucking a leaf

is akin to cutting
the throats of one
thousand monks.

*Here,* he says
*let me do that
for you —*

*how is this one?*

*Bhutan haiku*

on the road to Tiger's Nest
mistaking bird calls from Chinese tourists
as cries of pain

ascending the dusty path
my companion: the sharpened
walking stick

winded from altitude
knowing yet I will not
die I will not die

advised to arm myself
with a rock to guard against wild dogs
I discard the stone in a ditch

the duct-taped
prayer book, property
of the studious monk

animal hide glue binds
painted canvas to a temple wall
good merit for all sentient beings

rice grains in the window
seat at the temple
remnants of offerings

the strong man from Trongsa
turns his face away

when the medical aide
plunges the needle

into my upper arm,
the emergency room

bathed in morning light
where he brings me

when I slip and lose my footing
near the irrigation ditch

on the path to Chimi Lhakhang,
a landscape painted in phalluses

in the grainy streaming video
I watch his diminutive figure

contend in log dragging, wood chopping
heaving giant tires across a field

to secure an honor; the veteran
of war on the tour, our frailest traveler

falters, hobbled years ago
by a yacht injury, lucky to walk again,

he maneuvers with hiking poles
& when he tires, the strongman

carries the 235-pound grown-up
down the dirt path atop his back

to the edge of Sopsokha Village
when I turn back to look

he's holding the old man's hand
tending to those who can't move

as quickly, walking by my own side
on the ascent to Tiger's Nest,

he shares a dream of nearly finishing
engineering school, in his fourth year

to be expelled for an error made
in youth, I regard the tattoo on his

left arm that brings him regret
concealed beneath the sleeve

of his tartan gho, the pain
of old mistakes, to feel

one's worth, the might to strain
forward into the emerging

*The news of your death*

reaches me in the morning
a building crew across the street
pushes back their clamor

for an extra hour, rested
I rise to meet another day
stunned to see your face

flooding the internet
mourning messages burying
the story of what is known:

you ended your life;

three days after your body blackened
in a car you set ablaze by the rifle
range, you were named

in the local daily –
I lost no sleep at the gossip
of the Sakyong's sudden departure;

like father, like son –
the harm that cannot be undone
what I can't get past

the meaning in your last act
of resistance, the vows
we take as teaching

to do no harm, to do
no harm, to do
no harm

tonight, I think of Cid Corman
in Japan, a poet I never met

but who my classmate wrote to
two decades back taking

liberties he sent the aged

exile my poem, w/out
permission, which is also called

   "consent"

the elder sent his response by slow
boat and said "she might have

potential – a long way to go"
the poem – a text on practicing

tea ceremony, my name gave
me away as Asian – I'm sure

the white writer thought I'd find
his attention flattering as if

Ezra Pound himself had fingered me
as the next genius; last week

you learn the lineage holder
will return even after

such harm, the dictum

issued that only he will be
permitted to administer vows,

empower others; there are times
when we must part with tradition,

like ending that relationship
with the professor who sold

your letters to the archives,
never corrected his wife's

belief that you were
paramours, let it all burn

to the ground, let yourself
take up the teachings that you

already knew the day you
set foot in that classroom

*Shamanic*

when I hold the bronze
mold in my palm I see

the likeness of a menstrual cup
it's been a long spell since

I spoke to those ancestors

giving them the cold
shoulder for sending me chaos

disguised as a lover who called me
witch when his body erupted

in boils for his own betrayals,
it was medicine I asked for

when I invoked them in
the old-growth forest now

as I turn over the act of casting
108 miniature chortens I think of

what makes a gesture divine
to choose between Murphy's

soap and olive oil as standard
mold release, shoving a capsule

of ibuprofen into the clay body
or offering leaves of sage

what makes anything magic

[TO BE PERFORMED IN THE STYLE
OF DAVID ANTIN'S TALK POEMS]

[NOTE TO AUDIENCE: THIS TALK INCLUDES
A SECTION WHERE THERE IS NO TALKING]


On occasional Wednesday nights, I attend a Zen sitting
group that meets at St. Ignatius's chapel on the campus of
Seattle University. The chapel is an extraordinary work
of beauty, designed by celebrated architect Steven Holl.
During the day, each part of the chapel glows with tinted
light bouncing off color fields painted on the back of hung
baffles. As the days grow longer, the patterns of light entering
the chapel call out to the distracted eye untethered from the
meditation cushion. Sitting in this space has called forth
more than one poem.

## Sanctuary

the warning stick of the Zen priest
is a way to sharpen the mind

the parts of a soul we call back
to ourselves, baffled halos of light

in a stone box installed with seven vials
of radiance, we took our seats,

processing between pews and
through the hall of worship –

ceremony, a thing you shy away from
like the memory of Pentecostal rite,

the impulse, a desire, to recover
what was once whole, sunlight gunned

through colored glass the unbroken image
of St. Ignatius's shell reflected in the basin beyond

After sitting group one night, Tetsuzen, the group's resident priest, welcomed me to give a dharma talk, at any time, about any topic I might wish. I held my breath when he extended the invitation. I'm pure novice. Even after twenty-two years, I feel Impostor Syndrome rise up, take over my brain. It's reported that writers EJ Koh and Ocean Vuong spend hours of each day in meditation practice as their non-meditating petitioners marvel at this detail of their creative practice, agog in awe at the austerity of Asians. But I'm not that kind of Asian. I've got a six-year-old, and day-to-day life runs away from me. When the chemical reaction dissipates, I get curious about the idea of what it would be to give a non-dharma talk about my "feelings" about giving a dharma talk. And that is where we arrive now.

I take comfort in engaging in familiar patterns that move me a little closer to something that feels like perfection. Once, a designer built a poetry collection for me in such a way that it required that I hand cut holes in every book cover and hand stamp the interior of each book with notes about my text. We printed just under one thousand copies, which I prepped and cut in two weekends before shipping them off to my publisher's distributor. I went through a box of X-acto blades and a bundle of nail files, saving the letters from the words cut out of the covers to repurpose into personalized author notes. Contrary to what I imagined, the effect of reusing the text looked nothing like the roughness of ransom notes. I found the activity calming and embodied. I could be productive while thinking about nothing. Except when I saw my mind attaching too much to some idea of perfection.

## Practice

Pema Norbu Gompo
shares with me a story:
at reaching thirty

thousand prostrations,
glancing into the vanity
to see a trimmed down

waist w/out love
handles – starting over

from zero, more than once
to better polish his intent
my own practice:
carving holes in
poetry books

w/ X-acto blade & straight edge,
intervention as design concept

a hole too uneven
a hole too big
a hole too ragged
a hole too small

I've decided to embark on a new project that involves making exactly 108 clay *tsa-tsas* – Bhutanese sacred reliquary objects – that I'll give away. I view YouTube videos of street artisans and talk to clay artists about "standard release methods," including Murphy's Oil, corn starch, and olive oil. I read online tutorials, test different kinds of clay and wax, and also think about what could be placed inside the clay forms. In my readings on tsa-tsa making, I learn that medicine is sometimes placed inside these offerings. This is confirmed in one online video, when I see a tsa-tsa maker unceremoniously stuff what resembles an ibuprofen gel cap into a clay body. Somehow, I imagined more plantlike or magical healing medicine, even a handwritten mantra. My friend Michael offers to help me with my project, so I visit him in his ceramics studio that's a short dash from the college football stadium. A series of decisions unfolds before me about process: type of clay, glazes, firing temperatures. All of these possibilities also point to the specter of failure.

*Anything can go wrong, at any time.* Excess moisture in a preliminary firing can cause a piece to explode in the kiln. Too high a temperature can cause shattering. Glazing can behave unpredictably. And under particularly dramatic and expensive instances, a kiln shelf can blow up. We steel ourselves for the unpredictable. Make a backup cache of objects just in case. *Anything can go wrong, at any time* – like a mentoring relationship, or even a dharma talk that's lost control. We have to improvise. And this is the thing I think, as I wander the spice aisle of the University Village Safeway searching for pink Himalayan sea salt. Thinking about what desiccated herb might be a fitting offering to tuck away inside my clay objects, having forgotten the fragrant stems of Texas sage sitting atop my altar at home. There is no edible lavender to be found in the baking section.

[PAUSE TO MAKE TSA-TSAS FOR THREE MINUTES]

## All beings, our teachers

Calvin, the jazz poet, invited me to lunch
on the premise of electing me
for a poetry prize, when I arrived

for our meeting he opened the door
in his bathrobe, his apartment staged
with Orientalist porn

Evelina, the Asian American novelist
recruited me to teach without pay – I looked
the right part to a group of Pinay teens

she'd later take to Manila
as research subjects; when I
explained I needed work that paid

the rent she said I failed
in my responsibilities

the mentor Elise handed me a news clipping
from the *NY Times* –
here I am giving you a poem

the piece was on Vietnamese
tonal language speakers
why we have perfect pitch

I stopped learning Mandarin by the time I was eight
Now I am older, when I bump

into former instructors outside
the classroom they say

*She was my student.*
*She studied with me.*
*I taught her.*

For many years my best
teachers were books, they
would not force me with

calloused ashen hands, no
way of being misread
this aversion to learning

to teaching sometimes I miss
sharing my mind with others
in these moments I turn

to you and say claim this
beauty that belongs to you
and make it yours

We pack the clay into the three-inch molds that resemble menstrual cups. Apply gentle and firm pressure to ensure that the details on the inside of the molds imprint across the surface of the clay. The molds form miniature stupas, or temples. We tear off chunks and strips of clay from the base to form a standing foot that when brushed against a table or any texture takes on those notes. We knead and fold the clay into cones and bulbous tear-dropped shapes that more easily fit within the molds of the tsa-tsas. I watch Michael and his student Ren work the clay.

I haven't touched clay since I was a teenager. Ceramics was largely my older brother's domain. He partitioned off part of our parents' Southern California rambler and installed a pottery studio. He built containers on a rotating kick wheel and displayed his creations on rows of shelves lining the walls of the enclosed patio. I remembered the control he exerted over his fast-spinning, wet vessels, using not his strength but brute force. A reflection too of our own relationship.

No one tells me to handle the clay in a particular way. Both Michael and Ren explore their own relationship to the material. Rolling, pinching, tapping, peeling. I pick up some of their technique by watching and begin to understand that our task is to approximate a shape. Not the shape of the mold, but the more ambiguous shape of the thing that will fill the mold. It is hard to understand that these are different things. At times, the shape that emerges from my hands resembles something phallic, and embarrassed, I flatten my efforts into something squat, twist the clay into something geometrical. My mind tries not to fixate on the outcome of the perfectly formed tsa-tsa. Ultimately exerting more care versus being freer doesn't make a difference.

Michael starts splitting the clay into triangular shapes to improve our efficiency and production time per tsa-tsa. When I glance at the clock it's 10:40 a.m., but it's broken and fifty minutes later, the hands haven't moved. Tiny bits of dried clay stick to my hands. As I wipe them clean, Michael gestures at his typewriter suggesting all that can be transcribed and recorded from our conversations.

*What's the best technique to crimp the perfect new year's dumplings?*

Ask your Taiwanese sister-in-law.

*Who's given a memorable artist talk in recent Seattle history?*

Cedar Sigo on musicality and connecting to his indigeneity.

*What should be protected in the San Francisco Bay area?*

Cohen Alley, aka The Tenderloin National Forest, a throw-away space that was leased from the city by artists for $1 a month and transformed into an urban greenspace.

When the ribbon jammed on the Corona Electric, we abandoned technology for sharpie pens. The idea of reading to one another was tossed around but after counting only 103 completed objects, Ren and I doubled down to finish the job. Michael pulled out a Cooley Windsor essay to read aloud on the subject of teaching. Being read to as I created stirred an old memory of sitting in graduate school workshops laboring over a poem as the instructor fed lines to the class from abstract sources. The effect of listening to Windsor felt more akin to guided meditation. I didn't hate him. His work evoked tenderness. And the embodiment of that tenderness seemed bound to express itself in our last objects, in the close attention and fidelity to unformed matter molding to a shape. It is perhaps why some artists will also talk to clay as they relate to it. Like two lovers engaging with each other.

I gather up the molds that have enabled our work and oil and wipe the dried clay from inside and outside the bronze forms using an odorless yellow camellia oil. I complete the cleanup process three times, thinking of how the process of purifying and putting away your implements in Japanese tea reflects respect for the tools and an honoring of the spirit of servitude, hospitality, holding space for one another.

## Sangha

of the three jewels the most precious
is the community of practitioners,

I feel this truth acutely when I conjoin
with another disciple & we pivot to bow

in unison to the circle, as we retire
from sacred space, honoring how you & I

once turned toward a roomful of friends,
raised our hands to our hearts humbling ourselves,

to ourselves, I bowed with you, not to you
the gaze turning downward, my heart opened,

giving silent gratitude too for who we were then

In that space of mind meeting mind, the ancient ones and all the buddhas of the future stood present with us. And we were all awoken.

I am trying to hold the view that all spaces have the capacity to become sacred – the shell of a bronze mold acts as a womb. The writing desk, the uninhabited heart, the college lecture room. Even if who we were in that moment of first encounter will never again be who we are now, we brought our curiosity and reverence for what wasn't yet known. So that what starts as a "work party," something transactional, commonplace, with a goal of "being industrious," grows into something more joyful than a dinner party. That "productive aspect" is to be honored, the shared efforts of having toiled, sometimes failed, and found something together in the multifaceted gem, in spite of whatever breaks apart in the conduction of heat moving through a body.

*The uncarved block*

the thing we think
we want, perfection

to honor a fidelity
to origin when all

was ever in a state
of emerging

the soft bones forming
a newborn's skull

the fontanelle of the David's
marble crown left undone

imperfection a wholeness
complete unto itself

*Chubbies*

in the Punakha Valley of Bhutan
I came upon countless wall murals

of "flaming thunderbolts" adorning
the exteriors of stuccoed buildings

on the path to Chimi Lhakang
giant flying phalluses invoke

divinity, the holy man who was said
to have subdued a demoness

with his manhood, all of this
familiar I think, when he cuffs

me, awakening a want older than

the puerile boys of my youth –
they called them "chubbies"

those rococo painters reducing
desire to a caricature of a fat baby

eros: his shaft far more
lithe and lethal

*In the garden of Danny Woo*

I led you up terraced slopes
until we saw clear to Hing Hay Park

down Maynard Street, rattling
off the annals of Uncle Bob

how he leased the land
beneath our feet to feed

the elders, made
a thriving ecosystem where

there had only been neglect,
a plot of land covered in trash

& shattered glass restored to
life-giving beds of vegetables

through a shared belief in change,
fallen now into decay rain-soaked

winter leaves rotting underfoot,
the reports of sex trafficking

in massage parlors down the way
replete with unhappy endings,

you startle me from remoteness
when you pull me near, to quiet

speech, our tongues entwined in
some scattering of verdancy come alive

## Saline

*I lost my innocence*
*in water,* you say to me

when I was a child, no
more mature than five

that older boy who
knew better, alone

in the bath, beneath
bright fluorescent lights

his probing hands followed
by a twenty-year period

of forgetting &
an inexplicable terror

of death by drowning —

to clearly name now what
I leave behind in the brine

of Ala Moana, the sea
that has made me

her relative, he was
my brother,

someone I did not choose,
to trust, my own life

each day now remembering
this saltwater ceremony,

three immersions
this emergence

*Superstitious Asians*

if it were untrue, I might have been
less mad; I am the best of drivers

tiger mother, paper tiger, full
of slant, piss and vinegar

clamoring across a temple floor, divining
the silence of a question that no one ever

asked, friends and professionals lack
sound counsel because bias, no clues

to be found stuffed inside the metal
drawers of a Taoist shrine or

the images embedded within
a card drawn from the Ryder deck

just another kind of knowledge

to be cultivated "out there,"
a feeling akin at times to haunting;

I have looked upon my shadow,
argued with the ancestors,

peeling back the edges of my own heart
to show us both what's inside

*Imprints*

at the urban science museum
baby ducks fell into step

around us, as our bodies
cast shadows across pavement,

you invoked the fantasia of Disney
as I brooded over a more naked truth

we must not pet the wildlife —
such a fine line between

helping and harming

imprint of mother, what it felt like

to be held in loving tenderness &
its inverse — the rough touch of predator,

tearing the feathers out one
at a time, we learn the habits

of want at a young age,
the harm to self,

a script I choose
to now unwrite

*Cloisters*

after Oscar Wilde

in the seventeenth century, shoguns
installed *uguisubari* boards

in Nijo Castle, floors
that sing when cut across

like the trill of the nightingale
whose music was built by moonlight

& stained by its own heart's blood,
the squeak enough to drive any

man mad with walking on eggshells
nails mimicking the illusion

of passerine, in the royal
courtyard the roses scooped out,

replaced with peonies to cheat,
symbols of honor, romance

the happy ties that bind

*The pearl diver's tale*

after they recovered my body
from the brine, Prince Kamatari

plucked the pearl I hid inside
the slit I carved into my own

breast, snatched from
the Dragon King, the jewel

that possessed dominion
over tides and sea,

yet not her creatures –
the eight-limbed octopus

that ensnared me
in his embrace, followed

as I retrieved what
was precious, unlike

my other half
who could not

let me go

I looked beyond the boneyard
of crushed shells and half-eaten

creatures to see more than
a monster when they reached

toward me – the soft kiss
of sucking discs adhered to skin

to know the world as you do,
through touch, mimicking colors

of stone, sand, and seagrass,
to stroll across the ocean floor

with two legs, strange merfolk –
what spectrum of light do you

become asleep in your lair?
there next to me, six-armed

I beheld my own turns
of unconscious mind

if it's true that you
have three hearts

to whom did they belong?

when a limb is cut, what
memory does your body

continue to mourn?

what do you nurse
or remember besides
the deathlock of hunt?

is one heart the seat of consciousness
and the other the house of your soul
while the last pumps life through you?

does an octopus love any more
than a human can, grasp tight

to some memory of the maternal,
a potential mate, or to what is mutable

like the living glass of your own seeking?

*Embarkation*

butter lamp, incense stick, beeswax
votive, the occasion of poem, rites I enact

to set the world aglow with the light
of desire, the fire of the mind

adorned in the colors of the eight
temples, the caretakers of the wang yeh (gods)

march through the streets of the seaside town
the lone envoy bearing a square yoke, parades

the wooden boat through narrow lanes
until nightfall, when the barge is brought

to rest upon a bed of joss (paper)
earlier that night, men load the boat

with handwritten wishes, the misfortunes
and plague of the past year to be piloted

up to the heavens in a blast of fireworks
deafening the crowd that came to bear witness

to ceremony; we observe as each of us does
some of us bail out before a thing is done

to escape our ghosts; we watch it burn;
I can't unsnarl the knot of unmet want,

so I sever it in heat, draw the cord into flame
to free myself from the clutch of haunting, to disembark

at the latitude of where I give up the ship

*Virga*

as young people we are
taught to hold our tears

the feeling that could not
come to pass in the thundering

fallstreak, in piercing through virgae
we risk the jet plane flaming out

shafts of rain going sublime,
before ever touching ground

if this is dormancy, the self
unrequited, who would we be

if we became cloudburst?
consider the potted plant in the crook

whose roots could grow no deeper
its refusal to bloom & choosing

instead to shrivel; the lesson
now to pour down & resound

## Cuttings

at forty-five, my hands sink
deep into loam, clearing

room to plant propagated
stems given by a neighbor

grown in water that
trained *Tradescantia zebrine*

the wandering jew,

to get its needs met from
what was at reach, fragile

fibrous hairs, more
delicate than rootstock

transferred from earth
to potting soil, on that last

trip "home," I pinched a bit
of sand & soil from my uncle's

backyard in Ching Shui,
my father's homeland

brought back inside
a sealed bag in which

I wanted to imagine
we'd invent new roots

*Hongbao / white envelope*

*for Koon Woon*

Across the Chinese diaspora, our elders insert crisp new bills into miniature red envelopes to be shared with the young on the occasion of a new year, a birthday, a benediction.

These crimson gifts appeared on irregular occasions throughout my girlhood. If grades were high, if times were good. If the family business was net positive, that year.

As kids, we anticipated the amounts inside the gilded *hongbao* based on our performance of what qualified, or counted as good.

My parents retired trade after trade. We spent years living in the red. The failed shiitaki mushroom farm. The shuttered giftshop. An obsolete import business. We lived off credit.

As an adult, I catalogued the collections of a cultural museum and encountered the red envelope that I didn't see for decades. Unsure of the Chinese characters printed across its front, I asked my peer from the Mainland to confirm its use. She laughed. I didn't know the markings indicated its use for a wedding. Red with shame, I pictured a bride tucking the parcel into her cleavage.

When I stopped depositing his checks, I pictured my father growing red with ire. He found other ways to reach me. Posting unmarked envelopes of cash through the mail.

Imagining American dollars could be as secure a transaction as gold, the bills wouldn't expire or lose their exchange value.

The bachelor poet has sent funds to my son since he was two. He is not my boy's father. The twenty-dollar bills arrive enclosed within a plain white business envelope stamped with a chop. The image is of goldfish, transforming into yin and yang. No red ink, just black, just white. This note:

My father once told me that his sister in SF used to steal money from her gambler husband's trousers when he was asleep in order to send money to him in China when he was going to middle school. Those days, graduates of high school can become teachers.

*My father came to the US at 18 and worked in the Oakland naval shipyards.*

*He always told his children to go get the best education possible and that includes non-school learning as well. He was a practical man. I am not so much.*

*Enclosed is something extra for Tomo.*

*Best wishes,*

Koon

Before I was born, our surname had already been altered. The paternal grandmother mandated we take the bachelor's name for our own, to honor a relation outside the ancestral blood line. We were relatively new to the country then too, transplants from Fujian to Taiwan. The patriarch of our own family gone, it was the benevolence of a stranger that made life tolerable. No one got rich. Everyone had food to eat. From Tsai, we became Pai.

*Woon* is not your true name, any more than *Pai* is mine. We do not wear red or believe in luck. My ancestors were never at Gum Shan, nor were they present at the remembrance of the Golden Spike. We are biologically unrelated. Yet across dialect, generation, and clan, we do not ask whether we belong to one another. Like the koi that you choose to seal your stories, the connection to what's Chinese transmutes into care for all of our relations.

*Ashide no yo (garden poem)*

an Eastern red-eared terrapin
turtle moves with the pace of stone

the long crawl out of Lake Washington
into the daylight of Mapes Creek

site of an old stump farm
awakening a memory of land

clear-cut and harvested
in the time of the Heian

to imagine a woodland forest
where one was once removed

transformed by rock stood
upright to impart the heart spirit

horsetail rushes embedded
in a boulder, four billion years ago

permutations of the natural order
flow through weeping spruce

there in the cataract of blue atlas
water slapping against stone

an orange koi glides
alongside a choir of black carp

the bronze bell still throbbing

*Instructions for making earthworks*

after viewing Andy Goldsworthy

as beings that live
upon this earth we are

learning to relate to place;
leave a mark that's made

without the use of harm
rather than hack into bark,

or drawing into sand
leave an artifact behind,

something gathered
from the land to add

to what is already whole
a corona of flower petals

a snaking line of fallen logs
a row of stones curling into spiral

*Poems for an Aeolian harp*
*(or paintings for the wind)*

Gather a group of strangers.
Raise a strand of prayer flags together
to make an auspicious day.

Present a three-year-old
with a dandelion and pinwheel.
Let them choose.

Place a guitar where there
is wind. Let the breeze
play the open chord.

Exhale gently on a frigid day.
Notice your breath
as it touches your skin.

Let the wind move through
you. Color it with whatever tone
your voice wishes to imbue.

Steal the leaf blowing machine
from the landscaper. Take it aboard a boat
and hurl it into the sea.

Rake a pile of fallen foliage
and leave it where
there is wind.

*Columbarium*

write the epitaphs of those
you have lost on separate sheets
of spirit paper, fit the words
into the shape of each golden
foil, when you are done
char them to ash leaf by leaf

*Needle mass for a* Hari-Kuyo

pressed and tempered carbon
steel wire cut to the length of two

the seamstress' "soul mate" –
thread tethered through a sharp's

all-seeing eye, sacramental
pardoning of secrets, grief

interred in cormous cake rest,
tools embedded in tenderness

devil's tongue jelly berth burial

*Tidying up*

when I retire my son's well-worn
clothes to the consignment pile
I reach for the maternity outfits

stowed beneath the marriage bed
reconsider the hand-me-down dress
given to me by the Bellevue mom

who conceived again after
miscarriage, the nursing shirt
worn by my college roommate

after the birth of her boy,
the new dress I bought myself
on my nonprofit paycheck

things I can't let go, no
spark of joy, yet some other
category of worth,

invested with the energy of
an immutable line of mothers
the aura of fecundity,

garments that hum
with divine life, my child now five,
reaching toward gratitude

to give thanks for such

## The Century Building

in a silent bid to protect itself against
historic designation, the property

owners of 10 Harrison Street remove
the midcentury sun panels obscuring

office windows to alter the appearance
of Bystrom & Grecoof's post-stressed

concrete and brutalism
Pacific Northwest minimalism

made less to achieve a fuller market value
defensible as needed seismic improvement

the variance between a $3-4M swing
in sales price, board members raised

their hands to discuss stewardship,
fiduciary duty of an organization's

stakeholders – trading on imaginary
"children" – the real estate developer argued

"you can always build a building,
but you can't fulfill a kid's dream"

how a pass-through funder touches
the lives of disadvantaged youth

at a far distance, an abstract audience
easier still to picture than the Queen Anne

Historic Society – corporate types skirt
a motion to apply stucco atop brick exterior

to change a street-facing façade
further impairing landmark status

the occupants deafened by jackhammers

*Since form follows function*

during the Denny Regrade
property owners spurned

selling their plots forcing
those who re-engineered

the city to work around them
in that same vein, Edith

Macefield refused to surrender
her Ballard bungalow

to multistory mall developers
I contemplate grudges, bad blood

expressions of enmity
spite mounds, spite house

the acid of spite poem

*White savior industrial complex*

while reading a white activist's
book on civil disobedience

I encounter the passage of
that time he evaded Johnny Law

by hiding with his friends
in Yellow Face onstage,

the "wrong side of Murder Creek"

I think how activism, like feminism,
often fails people, like that time

175,000 protestors armed with
pussy hats marched through

the Chinatown on the eve
before the Lunar New Year,

without giving the community notice
ahead of time, never considering how

they'd close streets, affect traffic,
or impact business on what would

usually be the busiest weekend
of the year, even Uwajimaya

seeing a sharp drop in sales

*On ceremony*

an old crush sent me
porcelain dinnerware when

I married as if to mark
my entry into the society

of good wives; the plates
were yellow and had shattered

in transit from his home
in Las Vegas to my temporary

outpost – I said nothing
because like the plates

I am yellow, that is Asian,
we people pleasers of many

secrets, like how I learned
to hide what's outdated

like that hideous yi xing
tea pot my mother put out

every time the giver who
gave it comes to visit

*The International Children's Park gets a new name*

a year after Donnie Chin
guardian of the I.D.

is gunned down at 8th and Lane
city officials elect to change

policy: dead less than three years
managers rededicate the public park

in Donnie's honor, his murder

still unsolved, the park already
in its second evolution overhauled

four years before to increase a sense
of public safety – kids from

the neighborhood gave their two
cents on the redesign gathered

from the local daycare the namesake
of another casualty caught in the crossfire

of rival gangs nearly forty years ago
a friend of Donnie's, she tended the plots

that would become the district's open spaces –

Gene Viernes, Silme Domingo, Bob Santos,
Denise Louie: names we will not forget

a community garden sprouting
along Main Street where elders still raise

produce, the history of a district's
heart largely lost to public record

*Chiang-Kai Shek boneyard*

the streets have been renamed
by politicians to bear fewer
remembrances of colonial times
as society evolves to retire master

narratives; what would it mean
to my father and his generation
to regard this graveyard of the past
collected together in one memorial

park acres of bronze busts
all over the nation monuments
beheaded, spray painted with
graffiti or simply taken down

the Generalissimo as wounded
hero, the dictator riding out
on a dogged steed soldiers
salute each day in choreographed

displays of military honor for one
who lays putrefying in state
guarded by young men in white
uniforms who perform daily

acts of allegiance, forbidden from
taking photographs of the tomb
I focus instead on the twenty-year-old
cadets saluting the ruler who never

commanded them, sweating in the heat
of midday the vacant face of the recruit
his brow patted dry by a superior while
standing at something less than full attention

*The Gathering at the Orchid Pavilion*

Near the Michigan Ave. entrance
after looking for upward of

an hour, the poet asks at the info
desk where he can find the "orchid

pavilion," describing wooden pillars
a dimmed room, his mission met

with blank stares on his journey
he strode past sky blue celadon

crossed the threshold of a portal
seeking a place that he had

read about in her poems, but registered
the wrong name, having entered

into his own mountain while passing
by prints from Hokusai's *36 Views*

the peak seen best from a distance,
less apparent to the eye up close

*Zuihistu in four parts for Richard Serra*

## Monolith

in Utah, surveyors
find a metal pillar

inserted into public land;
bakers in Corona Heights

plant "the ephemeral edible"
a gingerbread column

discovered on xmas day

here on Duwamish land
Serra's steel sculptures

undulate along the edge
of the Puget Sound, made

out of an act of commerce
their installation wasn't kept

a secret, totemic forms
standing upright speak

a language of stones
moored in a Japanese garden

## Homeomorphic

a torus is just
a donut pulled

out of the geometry
of coffee mug

the ambient space
of deformation:

a ship's hull shrinks
down into a pillow-

shaped hard candy,
thread of sugar

stretching into
the hollow barrel

of a tube of pasta

# Collections of similar things

shafts of light mimic
rain falling at a slant

a metal face turned
toward the light,

sings to volcanic stone
profiles on Rapa Nui

abstracted figures
move with the energy

of the human spine
knees flexed, dancers

ready to leap

the Quaker Oats box –
the camera obscura

dark chamber
for the long exposure

## Panoramic

the mind enters
past twin gates

asking if the eye
can ever take in

the whole view
w/in a single glance

if there is
a method

to capturing
time's memory

is it to bracket light

*Star shine*

in the search for signs of intelligent life,
we are blinded by want of a twin

we measure flux, gunned through
a telescope, seeking the sun that comes

right at us, to shine its light upon
a distant world still unborn, but of

the mind bathed in starlight

in the search for signs of intelligent life,
we are blinded by want of a twin

her face turned toward you in resonance,
we plot confirmation from the spheres

that were there at birth, mapping the gap
between cosmos to astrum revealing mysteries

of atmosphere, chase heavenly transits,
in the search for signs of intelligent life,

we are blinded by want of a twin
here in the burning traversion of bodies

our positions sculpted by gravity, in an order yet
unnamed, the outlying being exits

in the search for signs of intelligent life,
we are blinded by want of a twin

*Lines written during a pandemic*

as a child I hated both
bananas and running, two
things that tasted bad,

took stubborn pride
in coming in last with
a fifteen-minute mile

now these doings are
part of a daily routine
tracking my potassium

intake, the slow rewiring
of the brain being rebirthed
as I count the strides

*Upaya*

we have loved
each other long
enough

that what I don't say still
echoes in the mind,
I am so bored

of raising facts:
stabbings, shootings, assaults,
my husband knows

better than to tell
me what to do, speaks
his care so that

I don't have to eat
my fear of going alone
to the grocery store

I have choices like
that day one month ago
when I asked my son

to please stop
telling people
we are Chinese

## Amnion

in the fluid of the womb before
human life pushes outward,

the memory is already etched with
the residue of each past spark

in another life, I was mother
in another life, I was man
in another life, I was beggar
in another life, I was heir

in another life, I lived through war
in another life, I was betrayed
in another life, I believed in a god
in another life, I saved myself

in another life, my life was claimed by hunger
in another life, my life was stolen by disease
in another life, my life was taken by poverty
in another life, my life was ended by violence

in another life, I died childless
in another life, I died without a name
in another life, I died alone

in this being reborn, the anamnesis
of past actions, this awakening from dormancy

# Eddy

caught in the spiral of time,
I circle swim through

another lap, advance one more
spoke on the amaranthine wheel

the flip turn a reversal
of direction by the swimmer

who repels against the walls
of an imaginary pool not grasping

that the lines and planes
of this four-sided geometry

has their limits beyond those
boundaries: open water

limitless sea

## Plunge

If 60 percent of our bodies
are made of water, does this account
for why human beings float?

If I think too hard, will I sink like a stone?

If skin is the largest and most permeable
organ of the body, who do I become when
submerged in saline?

If I experienced amnesia,
would I have to learn how
to crawl again?

Do you prefer to be reborn
as a woman, dolphin
or man?

Through which channel
do you hope to re-enter these tears?

If I wish to take hold
of water's meaning, what
would permit me to take that plunge?

## Tidal

the ocean bulges toward the moon
as wine decanted in a chalice

flows over a rim; the coastal edge
a liquid boundary; the planet's flood

tides guided by celestial mechanics;
in the moon, the rise and fall

of tidal surf, lunar phases pull
gravitational forces bring incoming

storm surges, orbital cycles of shedding
tsunami swells like scorched earth,

wash away corporeal traces of calcium,
sodium, phosphate, copper, and chloride

trappings, mineral and matter discharge

## Have you ever tried to bully a wave?

the roar of ocean drowns out
all other voices; until there is

nothing but the crash of brine
the chanty that we are all invited to hum

through the corner of my eye
I see it coming –

tally the seconds before wave's
next full crest, breathe through

the break, hold the deadlock
of time within the body,

knowing that motion is immaterial

ease into the place where
I can pull myself upright to standing

tides undulating beneath my cadence

*Elegy*

      *for Kristin Kolb*

At Doe Bay, we strip down beside each
other in a wood-paneled shack after
reading poems to each other all morning
I feel shy then, never having seen another
woman's chest after double mastectomy
remembering the cancer survivor who
described the removal of her nipples
as permanently shutting both eyes

we share the soaking tub
with a young couple possibly
in love; the will to live comes
and goes, both of us in retreat
you came to Orcas to heal
while I arrived in search of something
I can't name, each of us
apart from our kids, your daughter
my son, we recall the labor &
good work of mothering

as I quell the urge to comfort
when I learn how your child was taken
from you in divorce; I think back
to that day now when I read the news
of your death in the shallows
of the marina near the boat where
you made your home; on the eve before

you planned to rejoin the world
of the living, your body found by
a stranger, face down as if
Ophelia, wondering if you lost
the resolve to save yourself from sinking

*Point Lobos*

along the western waterfront
I froze while walking across
the ancient seawall

waves rising up against
the ruins of architecture
as around me perfectly styled

couples posed for wind-swept
engagement photos staged
in the calm of saltwater

reflecting pools mothers
hiking with newborns
wrapped to their chests

crowded the passageways
with utmost ease how they resembled
the young women in elaborate dress

who are effortless in ascending
the dusty path up to Tiger's Nest
babes strapped to their backs

hiking the Paro Valley
I felt anxiety then too
fear for my companions

the New Mexican rancher
with the hernia, the old woman
celebrating her seventieth year

the man with the enlarged
atria with whom I tour
the ruins of history now

who gives me
an outstretched hand
when I lose sight

of where I stand staring
at distant sea stacks converging
to reveal the heart's contours

*Phosphene*

for Noel Quinones

some images reside within
the body, the outline of a common

frog, that face peering out
from an ancient petroglyph

warming that cave wall,
the shape of the archipelago

where your parents were born
known to you for so long

as an abstract land mass
on a hand-drawn map,

how we claim a place
when we are of the diaspora

nonisland island people
*como el coqui, soy de aqui*

learning now to sing your own song
*noel noel, coqui coqui*

*Marine Science Center, Port Townsend*

after an hour of exploring
indoor touch tanks with our son,

my husband signals he's ready
to move on, though our two-year-old

lingers unready to plunge
a hand into cold pools or to go

home, he'd held back Kort's hand
from touching the spiked orange

sea cucumber, buried his face
in our arms when a crab sidestepped

nearer, but regarded the colorful feather
duster worms with a closer curiosity,

that made me question the urge
to survive, instincts that no longer

serve a purpose yet keep us
from pushing out beyond the comfort

of the cocoon, hands clasped
together, I watched him

ease our child's palm into sea
water to come into contact with

the purple tentacled tube worms
fan-shaped appendages pulled

back in a flash, fear transforms
into surprise, delight repeating

itself again and again, as our son
grows bolder with each reach

*First-grade math*

my six-year-old's brain
is broken by the equation
<3 + 3 = 14

to solve for heart
sub an X like a treasure
map, his father gives

an analogy with cookies
as I observe the confusion
multiply in my son's speech

b/c love is another language
b/c heart is not a fixed number
b/c my love for you is infinite

*Nuance*

before bed, Kort reads
to our son, from a book

on Egyptian hieroglyphics
names the shapes he sees

as "lump, curlicue, knife, and hook"

amused, the poet in me insists on
words like "mound" and "spiral"

remembering how a therapist
once gave a friend of mine a handout

listing dozens of different ways
to describe anger, fear, and love

my child wrestles the book
away from his father and says

"feather" while pointing to the shape
that someone mistook for a dagger

the hook is just a hook

the spiral, a snail shell or
nautilus, I assert to everyone

laughing, my boy noting
you are *happy* today, right now

*On the grounds of the Tsubaki Shinto shrine*

in Granite Falls, my boy encounters
the stone Magatama, the black

marble sculptural form reaches
back to ancient Japan, curved

jewel, one half of the Tao —

sun or moon —
all light all darkness

snake coiled tight, the curled
tail echoes the shape of human

embryo, primal recognition
of what you once were in the womb

compels him close enough to feel
the smooth stone beneath fingertips

quickly intensified into two-handed study
Tomo-e — the name we gave

means "wisdom"; "friend"; plus one
other answer we did not account for

nor know — this mark, comma-like
form for the great mystery

of life he touches

*Gruel*

simmered rice in bone
broth builds sinews

the first solids I feed
my infant son,

other mothers said
Cheerios sugared cereals

*give him your word he'll know*
*the taste of cheeseburgers,*

cake – & yet the whole
family's gone gluten-free

grueling, the first pablum
my father received

when his mother had
an abscessed breast,

a wooden stick dipped
in porridge what

he nurses in the absence
of milk supply, powder

food shortages in wartime
no longer in a state

of famine, I affirm
my own accord

on your birthday

        a chime sounds
             with the breath of a zephyr

            a golden gong shimmers
                with sound

        the bronze bell

tolls

            with twin clarity

        such that you

who are nothing but ears,

arrive wide awake

# NOTES

Rōhatsu is the Buddhist holiday that commemorates the day that the historical Buddha, Siddhartha Gautama (Shakyamuni), experienced enlightenment. It is observed on the eighth day of the twelfth lunar month.

Avalokitseshvara is the bodhisattva ("buddha-to-be") of infinite compassion and mercy and is also known to Chinese people as the goddess Guanyin.

Tiger's Nest, also known as Paro Takstang, is a sacred Buddhist site and monastery in Bhutan. It is where the Buddhist mystic Padmasambhava first brought Buddhism to the country from India.

"Trongsa dzongkhag nyagoe" is the official title for the strongest man in Bhutan, a title currently held by Sonam Tenzin.

"The pearl diver's tale" comes from a three-volume book of erotic ukiyo-e that was first published in 1814. Inspired by Hokusai's *Tako to ama,* this specific woodblock print is known as the artist's most famous shunga design.

Virga is a weather phenomenon best observed in arid places like southern New Mexico. It is rain that never reaches the ground, or water that isn't wet. Virga is derived from the Latin word for "twig" or "branch."

Ashide no yo, as described in the gardening manual the *Sakuteiki,* is the "Reed Style" of gardening that mimicked a painting style that concealed short messages, or were overwritten by poetry.

Hari-Kuyō is the Japanese Buddhist and Shinto Festival of Broken Needles that is celebrated by women in Japan as a memorial to all the sewing needles broken in their service during the past year.

"Tidying up" is inspired by Marie Kondo, the Shinto organizing phenom who is widely known for her book *The Life-Changing Magic of Tidying Up.*

At the time of this writing, the Century Building which is located at 10 Harrison Street in Seattle, Washington, has not yet been redeveloped for urban housing.

"The Gathering at the Orchid Pavilion" is the poet's private nickname for Gallery 109 at the Art Institute of Chicago. Would-be art adventurers are advised to inquire about the Tadao Ando gallery, not the "Orchid Pavilion." Designed by architect Tadao Ando, Gallery 109 features the museum's Japanese antiquities and occasionally displays the painting "The Gathering at the Orchid Pavilion."

"Star shine" is based on the research of American astrophysicist Brett Morris and his study of the possibilities for life on other exoplanets.

Upaya means "expedient means" or "skillful means" and is associated with the Noble Truth of right speech.

Kristin Kolb (1974-2019) died on March 31, 2019, at the Cayou Quay Marina in Deer Harbor on Orcas Island. She was a writer and journalist who signed her columns with a quote from Albert Camus, "Always go too far, because that's where you'll find the truth."

Point Lobos is located in western San Francisco at Land's End. The ruins of Adolph Sutro's public baths can be explored from Point Lobos.

El coqui is a small arboreal frog that is the national symbol of Puerto Rico and is frequently seen in Taino pictographic drawings.

"Utter" was written for my son Tomo's godfather, the writer and filmmaker Tom Gilroy.

With gratitude to Kevin Gick for giving me the image
that became the centerpiece of this book.

Thank you to artist April Gornik for generously granting permission
to use her painting *Virga* for the cover of this collection.

With deep appreciation to Lauren Grosskopf and Michael Daley
for shepherding this project to publication.

SHIN YU PAI is the author of several books, including *Ensō* (Entre Rios Books, 2020), *Aux Arcs* (La Alameda, 2013), *Adamantine* (White Pine, 2010), *Sightings* (1913 Press, 2007), and *Equivalence* (La Alameda, 2003). From 2015 to 2017, she served as the fourth Poet Laureate of The City of Redmond, Washington. Her personal essays have appeared in *City Arts, Tricycle, Seattle's Child,* and *YES! Magazine.* Shin Yu received her MFA from The School of the Art Institute of Chicago. She's been a Stranger Genius Award nominee in Literature and lives and works on the ancestral tribal lands of the Duwamish. For more info, visit www.shinyupai.com.

\* COLOPHON \*

Set in Poliphilus, which is a facsimile of the text of the
*Hypnerotomachia Poliphili,* after which it is named, published by
Aldus Manutius in Venice in 1499, using a type that had been cut by
Francesco Griffo. Poliphilus is an exact copy of fifteenth century
printing on handmade paper. So exact in fact that even the
original ink spread is reproduced.

The italics are set in Blado®, the name given to the italic
of Poliphilus. At the time when Francesco Griffo cut the roman that
was used as the basis for Poliphilus, the practice of making an
accompanying italic had not arisen. Designed by the calligrapher
Ludovico degli Arrighi, it was named after the printer Antonio Blado,
who had used it in 1539.